# LINLITHGOW
# PALACE

## A Historical Guide
## to the Royal Palace
## and Peel

Text by Denys Pringle

Designed by HMSO Graphic Design, Edinburgh

Principal photography by David Henrie

Reconstruction drawings by Harry Bland

The illustrations on pages 8–9, 11 and 16 are
reproduced by gracious permission of
Her Majesty the Queen

Grateful thanks for permission to reproduce
other photographs to:

Cadw (Welsh Historic Monuments) (page 5)
The Dean and Chapter, Lincoln Cathedral (page 4)
The Duke of Hamilton (page 16)
The Duke of Roxburghe (page 4)
National Galleries of Scotland (pages 6, 8, 10, 14, 16, 17, 22)
National Portrait Gallery, London (pages 9, 18, 20, 23)
Royal Commission on the Ancient and
Historical Monuments of Scotland (pages 11, 20, 22)
Royal Museum of Scotland (pages 8, 11, 16, 17, 22)

**HISTORIC SCOTLAND**

Historic Buildings and Monuments

Edinburgh
Her Majesty's Stationery Office

# KEY TO BUILDING PERIODS

- ■ James I 1424–37
- ■ James III 1460–88
- ■ James IV 1488–1513
- ☐ James V 1513–42
- ■ James VI 1618–24

## Ground level

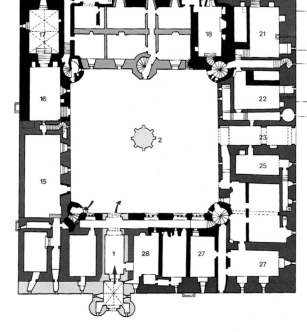

**Basement level**

**First-floor level**

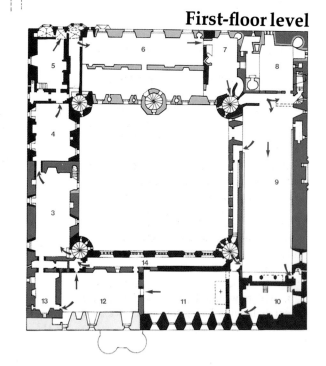

**MAIN TOUR**
**Number Key**
1 South Gate
2 Fountain
3 King's hall
4 King's presence
5 Bed-chamber
6 Long gallery/dining hall
7 Pantry
8 Court kitchen
9 Great hall
10 Withdrawing rooms
11 Chapel royal
12 Ante-room
13 Corner-tower
14 Gallery/transe

# A TOUR OF THE PALACE

INFORMATION BOARDS placed throughout the palace describe each room in turn and allow visitors to guide themselves around the building. Those who are pressed for time or who are making their first visit to Linlithgow, however, may wish to follow the recommended route described below:

Visitors will have entered the palace through the **south gate (1)**, built by James V around 1535. This leads into the central courtyard, the centrepiece of which is the elaborate **fountain (2)** dating from around 1538. Each façade looking into the courtyard presents a different building period: on the east, the **great hall** and the **original entry** of James I; on the south the English-looking **transe** of James IV and Margaret Tudor; on the west, the **state apartments** begun by James III and finished by James IV; and on the north, the 'New Work' constructed for James VI between 1618 and 1624.

The south-west turnpike stair leads up to the **king's hall (3)** on the first floor. This forms, with the **king's presence (4)** and **bed-chamber (5)**, a suite of royal apartments built for James III and James IV, with a similar suite for the queen located on the floor above. James V and Mary Queen of Scots would probably have been born in the queen's bed-chamber, in the north-west tower.

A modern catwalk now leads through the wrecked shell of James VI's **long gallery** or **dining hall (6)**, in the north range; only the finely carved fireplaces now give any indication of the former richness of the interior. Next we pass through the **pantry (7)**, up a few steps of the north-east **turnpike stair** and along the **service passage** into the **court kitchen (8)**, which would have served both the great hall and, later, the smaller dining hall in the north range.

The **great hall (9)** is the largest room in the palace and the grandest, built originally for James I (c1425) and later remodelled, notably by James IV. The **portcullis** of the main gate was formerly operated from a gallery within its west wall. To the left of the grand fireplace, a small door leads to a pair of **withdrawing rooms (10)**, each with its own garderobe.

After this, the next main room to be reached is the **chapel royal (11)**, begun by James IV and completed by James V. Note the angels, playing on different musical instruments, which decorate the niches between the windows. Beyond the chapel is an **ante-room (12)** and, finally, the south-west **corner-tower (13)**, containing a succession of **private chambers**, one above the other. Before going back down the **spiral stair** to the courtyard, have a look inside the **gallery** or **transe (14)**, which contains a small collection of sculpture and artefacts from the palace.

This completes the main tour of the palace, but visitors may wish to explore the following rooms in whatever order they choose:

**15–17 Cellars**
**18–19 Larders connected with the kitchen**
**21     Lower kitchen**
**22     Brewhouse**
**23     The 'Old Entry' of James I**
**24     The 'Outer Bulwark' or barbican of James IV**
**25     Guard-room**
**26     Prison**
**27     Stables**
**28     Guard-house for the 'New Entry' of James V**
**=     Queen Margaret's bower** may be reached up the north-west turnpike stair.

King Edward I of England.

King David I (and on the right his grandson Malcolm) from a charter granted to Kelso Abbey in 1159.

The palace and peel from the north-west.

# ROYAL RESIDENCE AND ENGLISH CASTLE
## (1150-1424)

**L**INLITHGOW LIES roughly midway between Edinburgh and Stirling, and 6 km south-west of Blackness harbour. The ruins of the palace stand beside St Michael's parish church on a natural hillock, which overlooks the town to the south and extends as a promontory into Linlithgow loch on the north.

A royal manor house probably existed on this site from the mid-twelfth century, when King David I founded the burgh and granted the parish church to St Andrews Cathedral Priory. The earliest certain reference to it, however, is made in November 1301, when the 'King's Chamber' was prepared for Edward I of England, whose army had invaded Scotland in support of John Balliol's claim to the Scottish throne.

Linlithgow's position made it an ideal site for a military base, and the following year the English king set about transforming it into a secure stronghold. The construction work was directed by Master James of St George, whose achievements already included the series of massive stone castles by which Edward had secured his conquest of Wales a few years before. The castle at Linlithgow, however, was more modest than these and was built almost entirely of earth and wood. The promontory was cut off from the town by a deep ditch, behind which was erected a *pele*, or stockade, made of split tree trunks. In the centre of this was a defended gatehouse, and at either end a wooden tower rose from the waters of the loch. Inside the *pele*, the stone church with its tower was also strengthened and converted into a storehouse. Finally, another ditch and palisade, slighter than the first, were constructed around the promontory to defend the castle against possible attack from the loch. This work was finished by the end of 1303; and during the siege of Stirling Castle, in 1304, the English were able to use it as their main supply base. On one occasion, 21 waggon-loads of timber, lead counterweights and stone ammunition for mangonels (stone-throwing siege artillery) were sent from Linlithgow to the English camp at Stirling.

Linlithgow was still being garrisoned by the English in 1309, and Edward II spent at least a week there in October 1310. But after the battle of Bannockburn, in 1314, it returned to Scottish hands. The chronicler Barbour describes how a local man, named William Bunnock, smuggled eight men into the castle hidden in a cartload of hay; it seems as likely, however, that the English garrison simply abandoned it on the approach of Sir James Douglas. In 1337, King David II granted the 'peill' to John Cairns with orders to build it up for the king's coming. This he evidently did, for David held court there in 1343 and in later years. Repairs to the king's 'house' or 'manor' are also recorded during the reign of David's successor, Robert III (1390–1406).

Of the early manor house and castle nothing remains except the name, the 'Peel', which today is applied to the whole of the Royal Park surrounding the palace. Walking around the promontory, however, it is not hard for visitors to imagine the vast military entrenchment that once enclosed it.

The gatehouse of Harlech Castle in North Wales, built by James of St George for Edward I, 1283–90.

Rhuddlan Castle in North Wales, built by James of St George for Edward I, 1277–82.

# THE ROYAL PALACE OF JAMES I
## (1424-1437)

James I, by an unknown artist.

IN 1424, a disastrous fire destroyed most of the town of Linlithgow as well as the parish church and the royal manor house. King James I, who had only recently returned from exile in England, set in train almost at once a programme of building work, which, little more than a century later, came to completion in the royal palace much as we see it today.

The first campaign of works ran from 1425 until the king's assassination in 1437. By 1430, some £2440 Scots are recorded as being spent by John de Waltoun, the Master of Works; and, by June 1428 the place was habitable enough for the king to spend some days there. Payments to masons, carpenters and sculptors in wood and stone are recorded in 1430–1; and in 1434 the accounts include a payment for supplying colours to Matthew, the king's painter, suggesting that the sculpture, ceilings and wall-plaster were being decorated in the fashion of the day. A high rate of expenditure was maintained until the start of 1437, when work ceased abruptly on the death of the king.

The inner end of the gate passage to James I's palace, formerly surmounted by statues representing the Three Estates: the Clergy, Lords and Commons.

*Far right:*
The great hall, which despite later modifications and eventual ruination still gives a vivid impression of the grandest room in James I's palace.

While the documentary sources give a good indication of the amounts being spent by James I on his new palace, they give few details about the nature of the work being carried out. Examination of the building itself, however, suggests that work was concentrated on what are now the east range, including the great hall, and the adjacent parts of the north and south ranges. The palace would thus have had a C-shaped plan, probably open on the west.

The main entrance was on the east, and was approached along a lane passing around the east end of St Michael's church. The grandiose gateway in the centre of the palace's east wall still survives, though the ramp and drawbridge before it have long since gone. Above it in a rectangular panel are the royal arms, supported by a pair of angels and surmounted by another angel with outstretched wings. To either side are canopied niches, intended to hold large statues, perhaps of St Andrew and St James. Between these and the central panel are the vertical slots that would have held the gaffs from which the drawbridge was suspended.

The principal room of the new palace was the great hall, situated on the floor above the gateway in the east range. This ranks as one of the finest medieval interiors in Scotland, though in its present form it dates largely from the reign of James IV. The hall of James I, however, would have been little different in scale, measuring internally some 9 by 30 m, with clearstorey windows high up in the walls and a wooden roof. At the north end, beyond the screens passage and servery, lay the large kitchen, square in plan with a high vaulted ceiling (possibly with a flue for the escape of smoke and fumes at the centre). The royal apartments were probably situated in the south range, where they would have been easily accessible from the upper or high-table end of the hall and where evidence of domestic apartments is provided by a blocked latrine chute and a chimney in the later chapel wall. Documents of 1427 also refer to work on the park and fish ponds.

The gateway to James I's palace, surmounted by the royal arms.

The east front of the palace, showing the gateway of James I.

James II, by an unknown
artist.

The lower, or meat kitchen,
which originally consisted of
two rooms, one above the
other.

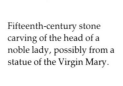

Fifteenth-century stone
carving of the head of a
noble lady, possibly from a
statue of the Virgin Mary.

A medieval tombstone,
probably from St Michael's
kirkyard, re-used as
building material in the west
range.

Doune Castle.

# THE PALACE UNDER JAMES II AND JAMES III

## (1437-1488)

A painting (by an unknown artist) of Henry VI of England, who stayed at Linlithgow in 1461.

J AMES II (1437–60) was only seven years old when James I was murdered at Perth, and it is not until July 1446 that there is any record of him taking an interest in his father's palace at Linlithgow. Over the next few years a number of small payments were made for repairs, mostly to the roofs, but also to the fish ponds and nets, the park ditch and stables. In 1450–1, repairs were also made to the palace enclosure. But the king seems to have made little use of the palace before his death at Roxburgh in August 1460, when an exploding cannon severed his leg.

His son, James III (1460–88), was also only a boy when he came to the throne. In 1461, however, there is mention of the king's Arras tapestry being taken from Falkland Palace to Linlithgow; and in the same year the keeper, John of Kincade, made some necessary repairs for the reception there of the fugitive King Henry VI of England. The palace, therefore, seems to have been used as a residence from early in the young king's reign. In the following years some small sums were also spent from the Exchequer on repairs to the floors and roofs. In 1465 these included the repair and roofing of a new kitchen; the construction of a kitchen is also mentioned in 1469–70. Possibly it was at this time that the lower kitchen, beneath the main kitchen serving the great hall, was remodelled by demolishing the vault that had previously divided it into two.

In 1469, James III married Margaret, the daughter of Christian I of Denmark, and both Linlithgow Palace and Doune Castle were included in her marriage portion. More substantial building works are recorded around this time, £518 9s being spent by the Master of Works, Henry Livingstone, between June 1469 and October 1470.

It is not entirely certain, however, which parts of the palace these new works affected. It may have been at this time perhaps that the south range was extended further west to terminate in the high corner-tower which still stands at the south-west corner. Related to this development, though structurally secondary to it, was the block containing the king's hall and a now-destroyed turnpike stair in the angle between it and the south range. If all these works or even merely their foundations can be attributed to James III, it would appear that the plan to enclose the west side of the palace already existed before the accession of James IV in 1488.

James III (far left) and his Queen, Margaret of Denmark (left), as they appear on the altarpiece painted for Trinity Church, Edinburgh, by the Flemish master Van der Goes (now in the National Gallery of Scotland).

9

# THE BUILDING WORK OF JAMES IV
## (1488-1513)

James IV, by an unknown artist.

A unicorn decorating the ceiling in the king's apartment.

QUEEN MARGARET DIED in 1486, and her husband, James III, was killed on 11 June 1488 while fleeing the battlefield at Sauchieburn. Their son, James IV, came to the throne at the age of 15, and almost at once assumed the reins of government. In the first year of his reign, the accounts of the Lord High Treasurer record 5s being spent to send a carpenter from Dundee to inspect the palace work at Linlithgow. From this it appears that construction was already in progress; and, from the recorded works that followed, it becomes clear that the young king had decided from the very start of his reign to transform Linlithgow Palace into a modern royal residence. By the time of his death in 1513 the transformation was virtually complete.

The west range, completed by James IV.

The three-storeyed transe of the south range (with the 'new entry' and fountain added under James V).

The most significant element in the new work was the completion of the new west range, closing off what had formerly been the open side of James I's palace. This new range contained suites of royal apartments for the king and queen. The new works, however, affected the whole palace and not only this new construction. The great hall was remodelled with new clearstorey windows, re-roofed and possibly enlarged. The kitchens, brewhouse, larders and pantry were renovated; and, although only fragments of it now survive, works were also carried out on the north range.

In the south range, the south-east corner-tower was completely rebuilt above ground-floor level. Immediately west of this, a new chapel was constructed at first-floor level, where some of the royal apartments had probably been before. And a three-tiered transe, or enclosed gallery, was built on the north side of the south range overlooking the central court, to link the great hall with the new west range. The peculiarly English style of this façade is perhaps the result of English masons working on the palace, following the King's marriage in 1503 to Margaret Tudor, the daughter of King Henry VII of England. At that time Linlithgow Palace was settled on the queen as a dower house, along with other properties including Doune Castle and Stirling Castle.

The west range from inside the courtyard, as completed by James IV.

On 9 September 1513, the peace with England having foundered, James IV faced the earl of Surrey's army on Flodden Field, where he fell along with many of the Scottish nobility. Queen Margaret is reputed to have waited vainly for his return from the battle in the draughty look-out post above the north-west turnpike stair, known today as 'Queen Margaret's bower'. Although Linlithgow still belonged to the queen, in 1514 she married Archibald Douglas, sixth earl of Angus, and fled Scotland with him the following year.

The top of the stairway to the royal apartments, showing the intertwined initials of James IV and Margaret.

*Above:*
A glazed tile from the king's presence chamber bearing the monogram of James IV and Margaret Tudor.
*Left:*
Margaret Tudor, the wife of James IV, from a portrait by Mytens in Holyrood Palace.

The vaulting of the passage next to the king's closet.

The closet and oriel window adjoining the king's bed-chamber.

The king's bed-chamber as it might have been at the time of James IV.

*Above:*
The king's presence chamber as it might have been at the time of James IV.

*Left:*
The Chapel Royal.

*Right:*
The king's presence chamber as it is today.

The remains of the barbican today.

The 'Outer Great Bulwark' or barbican, added to the east side of the palace by James IV.

# THE ROLE OF THE ROYAL PALACE IN THE AGE OF JAMES IV

A ROYAL PALACE in the late middle ages served not only as the monarch's residence; for in addition to the practical problem of housing and feeding all the members of the royal household a palace also played a more symbolic role by providing a setting in which political power could be displayed. To the king's subjects political power depended almost entirely on personal contact with him; and for this reason, access to the king was carefully controlled. The way in which this was done can be seen most clearly in the architectural layout of the new suite of royal apartments which James IV built for himself and for his queen, probably completing an earlier programme begun by his father.

The king's and queen's suites occupy the west range of the palace, the king's on the first floor, the queen's on the second. Each includes an outer hall, a throne room or presence chamber, and a bed-chamber; and the king's also had a small private closet. Only the closest of James's personal friends would have been invited into the closet; with its fine vaulted ceilings decorated with unicorns, this was essentially a private room, in which he could relax or gaze out through the large bay window over the loch. The bed-chamber, on the other hand, had a more public character than one would associate with such today, for it was also used as a private sitting room. Here the king would have discussed important matters of state with his ministers and counsellors; and below the floor was a strongroom, which would have contained the treasury when the king was in residence. In the presence chamber next door, the king would have been seen by the more important of his subjects or by visiting ambassadors in a formal setting as head of state, seated upon the Throne or Chair of Estate beneath a richly decorated canopy, with the Cloth of Estate displayed behind him. Beyond this room was the outer hall, in which the royal guard was stationed to control access to the sovereign.

Another important aspect of medieval kingship was the perception of the sovereign as a ruler designated by God, symbolised in the coronation ceremony by his anointment with oil in the manner of Old Testament priests. The new royal chapel, begun around 1490, was therefore a significant feature of James IV's new palace; and it is likely that the decoration of its painted and carved stonework and woodwork, its stained-glass windows and its glazed floor-tiles would have emphasised the king's special relationship with the Almighty. In 1513 an organ was installed by a Frenchman named Gilyem (William). The king and queen would probably have attended services in the royal pew located in a gallery, or loft, above the heads of the rest of the congregation and accessible from the transe leading to the royal apartments.

Finally, the king was also the nation's leader in war; and although for James IV, as for his father and grandfather, this was to prove his undoing, a royal palace was also expected to reflect the martial aspect of royalty. Lists for jousting and butts for archery were therefore provided in the park. But, while the other royal palaces at Stirling and Edinburgh were situated inside castles, the palace of Linlithgow at this date was hardly fortified at all. It was probably to rectify this shortcoming and create an impression of castellated grandeur that James IV's builders constructed in front of the east wall a turreted barbican, similar in appearance to the 'Foir Front' of the same period at Stirling. But while James's new defences at Stirling served a valuable military function, here at Linlithgow they were no more than an elaborate sham, for the other sides of the palace were left virtually defenceless.

Angels in the Chapel Royal.

# THE COMPLETION OF THE PALACE BY JAMES V
## (1513-1542)

James V who was born in Linlithgow Palace, 10 April 1512 (painting by an unknown artist).

The fountain in the centre of the palace, built around 1538.

**B**EFORE THE TEMPESTUOUS events which saw the demise of James IV and the removal, albeit temporarily, of his queen, Margaret had given birth in Linlithgow Palace, on 10 April 1512, to a son, who now at 17 months succeeded his father as James V. It was not until 1528, however, that the young king finally freed himself from the control of the various regents who had ruled Scotland during his minority. During these years, little mention is made of Linlithgow Palace, and it seems that for most of the period it stood empty and disused.

In 1526, however, a new captain and keeper of the palace and park was appointed, Sir James Hamilton of Fynnart; and, in March 1534, the mason Thomas French began work on the palace building. Thomas French came from a family of masons, probably, as the name suggests,

Over the outer gate are the arms of the four orders of chivalry to which James V belonged: the Garter of England, the Thistle of Scotland, the Golden Fleece of Burgundy, and St Michael of France.

originally of French origin. His father, John French, seems to have worked on St Michael's church in Linlithgow, where in 1489 he was buried in the newly completed north aisle. Thomas's son, also named Thomas, was buried in Aberdeen cathedral in 1530, in the aisle which father and son had just built for Bishop William Elphinstone. The revival of work at Linlithgow, however, drew Thomas senior back into the royal service as master mason of the new works. Indeed, he was already working in Linlithgow as master of the 'kirk work' in 1532, when he made an agreement with the town council concerning the battlements of the new choir.

The detailed building accounts kept by Sir James Hamilton and Sir Thomas Johnston, the king's chaplain, provide vivid details of the works being carried out in these years. The main entrance to the palace, inconveniently situated on the east side, was moved to the south, and an outer gateway was built south of it, giving access to the outer enclosure from the town. The proportions of the south front were also improved by straightening out the south wall and enlarging the south-west tower to balance the one on the south-east. In the chapel a new wooden ceiling and canopied altarpiece were inserted, the interior was painted and the windows re-glazed with painted images. The great hall was refurnished and given new windows; alterations were made to the kitchen; and the external sculptures were painted. The fountain in the centre of the court was built around 1538; and in 1540 there is reference to a catchpull, or tennis court, similar to the one still surviving at Falkland Palace.

James V's queen, Mary of Guise-Lorraine, whom he married in 1537, is reported to have compared Linlithgow Palace to the noblest châteaux in France. Nevertheless, like the palaces at Stirling and Falkland, Linlithgow was a monument to James's extravagant tastes. But his intemperance in other matters was to have more serious consequences. In August 1540, the keeper of Linlithgow, Sir James Hamilton, was executed on trumped-up charges, principally, it was said, so that the king could acquire his large personal fortune. Finally, after the disaffection of many of the Scottish nobility and the routing of his army by the English at the battle of Solway Moss in November 1542, James withdrew, a broken man, to Falkland, where he died on 14 December, only six days after the birth of a daughter, Mary, to the queen at Linlithgow.

St Michael's Church, built at the same time as the palace, between 1424 and c1535.

*Below left:*
The Chapel Royal at Linlithgow, as it might have appeared at the time of James V.

The south front of the palace as it might have been when completed by James V.

A sixteenth-century red woollen hanging, with applied black silk, embroidered with golden yellow silk, which is believed to have come from Linlithgow Palace.

*Right:*
Mary Queen of Scots, born in Linlithgow Palace, 8 December 1542.

*Far right:*
James Hamilton, duke of Châtelhérault and second earl of Arran, in a painting by Arnold Bronckhorst.

The bed-chamber of Mary Queen of Scots, in Holyroodhouse, which gives an indication of how the palace rooms at Linlithgow may once have looked. The painted frieze and ceiling date from 1617 and the Flemish tapestries from the later seventeenth century.

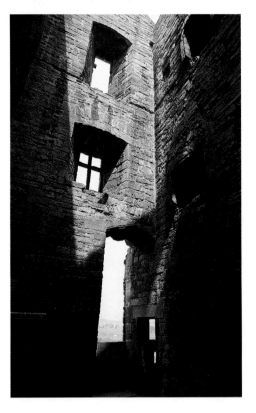

*Right:*
The queen's bed-chamber, the birthplace of James V in 1512 and of his daughter, Mary Queen of Scots in 1542, was probably located on the floor above the king's bed-chamber, in the north-west tower of the palace.

# THE PALACE IN THE TIME OF MARY QUEEN OF SCOTS
## (1542-1585)

A wooden ceiling-boss, such as might have decorated one of the royal apartments around 1530.

L INLITHGOW PALACE is perhaps best known as the birthplace of Mary Queen of Scots. Yet Mary was not the only Scottish monarch to be born in the palace, for her father, James V, had also been born there, probably in the same room, the queen's bedchamber situated in the north-west corner-tower. Nor was Mary's association with Linlithgow anything like as close or as fruitful as those of her predecessors or immediate successor, whose building works may still be admired. As it turned out, the infant queen remained only seven months at Linlithgow before being taken by her mother, Mary of Guise, to the greater security of Stirling Castle. It was another 20 years before she returned and almost half a century before Scotland again enjoyed the benefits of a strong monarchy.

During these years, various small expenditures made on the palace, including the repair of windows (1543), the removal there of two iron gates from Holyroodhouse (1544), and the replumbing of the fountain (1545–6), indicate that some attention was still given to its upkeep by the government, headed by the Lord Governor, James Hamilton, second earl of Arran. In 1551, the palace was set aside for use by the queen mother, Mary of Guise. But it is the Lord Governor's lodging, located perhaps in the north range, which receives particular mention in the accounts. Stone was supplied for the Lord Governor's works in 1550, and lead and tin for glazing in 1551. In 1551–2, a total of £5268 was spent on works at Edinburgh, Linlithgow and the houses of Hamilton and Arran. New windows were provided for the Lord Governor's lodging in 1552, and the interiors were decorated by the painter Watte Bynnyng. The courtyard was repaved and, the following year, two new chimneypieces were installed.

Mary of Guise, who was given the palace as her personal residence in 1551 (painting attributed to Corneille de Lyon).

The young Queen Mary returned from France in August 1561, following the death of her husband, King Francis II. The palace and its surrounding park and garden appear to have been kept in reasonable repair during the years of her brief personal rule, when she also occasionally resided there; but after the accession of her infant son, James VI, in 1567, when Scotland was ruled once more by a succession of regents, the buildings and park were sadly neglected.

In September 1571, the keepership of the palace was granted to Captain Andrew Lamby, who installed himself in it with a garrison of 24 soldiers. Various important prisoners were warded in the palace at this time, including, in 1579, the insane third earl of Arran and his mother.

# THE PERSONAL RULE OF JAMES VI
## (1585-1625)

A window head on the north range, bearing the monogram of King James VI of Scotland.

James VI of Scotland (I of England), in a painting by Daniel Mytens, 1621.

**B**Y THE TIME that King James VI was old enough to assume control of the government in 1585, the years of neglect at Linlithgow were beginning to affect seriously the stability of the palace. Captain Lamby was replaced as keeper in December 1580 by Lord Robert Stewart, who had earlier been a prisoner there. In 1582, a new gardener was appointed, because the yards, orchards and gardens had long lain waste. And in the following May, Sir Robert Drummond, the Master of Works, reported that £100 would be required to repair the west quarter of the palace, which was 'altogidder lyk to fall down', or £1000 if his warning went unheeded. Parliament met in the great hall in 1585. But a letter to Sir Robert Cecil from the English agent, George Nicholson, in February 1599 reported, 'there is a quarter ruinous and the rest necessary to be repaired'.

It seems, however, that nothing was

*Right:*
Anne of Denmark (painting by Paul van Somer)

*Far right:*
The north range, built between 1618 and 1624.

done, for in 1607 the keeper, Alexander Livingstone, first earl of Linlithgow, reported to the king:

> 'this sext of September, betwixt thre and four in the morning, the north quarter of your Majesties Palice of Linlythgw is fallin, rufe and all, within the wallis, to the ground; but the wallis ar standing yit, bot lukis everie moment when the inner wall sall fall, and brek your Majesty's fontan'.

He added that he would have been to blame if he had not informed the king about the state of it two years before. It was to be another 11 years, however, before the king's officers began to repair the damage.

The north range was finally rebuilt under the direction of the master mason William Wallace, and represents, even in its present ruined state, one of the finest Renaissance façades in Scotland. It was begun in 1618 and completed in 1624. The symmetrical organisation of the exterior was mirrored in the planning of the interior. Four floors of living accommodation above a storage basement allowed for 14 sets of two-roomed apartments, opening off central corridors served by the central stair-turret. The first floor also contained, on the side overlooking the loch, a new long dining room or gallery, conveniently situated between the royal apartments in the west range and the kitchens in the east; further floors of

accommodation for courtiers and officers were also provided above the kitchen and pantry. In the following years repairs were also made to the great hall, chapel, fountain and the royal apartments themselves.

In 1589, Linlithgow and Falkland Palaces had been settled on James's queen, Anne of Denmark. But in 1603, on the death of Queen Elizabeth I of England, the court moved to London. The new palace buildings at Linlithgow, built after the Union of the Crowns of Scotland and England, were evidently intended to provide fitting accommodation for the enlarged court that would have accompanied the king when he returned to visit his native land. As it turned out, however, James did not visit Linlithgow when he returned to Scotland in 1617; and it was not until the reign of his son, Charles I, that a ruling sovereign again set foot inside the palace.

A window head on the north range, bearing the monogram of King James I of England.

A decorated bone plaque from the stock of a long gun of around 1600, discovered in excavations below the west range in 1987.

The long gallery in the north range.

*Right:*
Charles I (painting by Daniel
Mytens, 1631).

*Far right:*

Oliver Cromwell(painting
after Samuel Cooper 1656).

Linlithgow Palace as
illustrated by Capt J Slezer
in *Theatrum Scotiae* (1678).

*Right:*

Charles II (painting by the
studio of J M Wrlght,
*c*1660–5).

*Far right:*

James VII and II, who as
duke of York stayed in the
palace while Commissioner
to the Scottish Parliament
(painting by Sir Godfrey
Kneller, 1684–5).

# CHARLES I AND THE LATER STUARTS
## (1625-1688)

Lead glazed jug and delftware drug jar of the late 17th century found in the palace.

TWO SETS OF ACCOUNTS for Linlithgow prepared by the Master of Works survive from the reign of Charles I (1625–49). The first, for 1628–9, followed the appointment in August 1627 of Alexander Livingstone, second earl of Linlithgow, and his heirs to the keepership of the palace, and related to a projected royal visit which in the end never materialised. The works, costing £1400, lasted about eight months, and beside general repairs throughout the palace included the painting of the king's apartments by John Binning and James Warkman, and the painting and gilding of the carved detail on the façade of the new north range and on the outer gate.

In 1633, the accounts from March to the end of June describe a scene of intense activity, for on this occasion the king's visit was imminent. Earlier, in January, those living in the palace had been told to remove themselves and their belongings. The chimneyheads of the king's apartments were rebuilt, floorboards were renewed, the kitchens were cleaned out and put in order, windows and doors were repaired, and temporary stabling built. Matting was provided for the rooms of the Lord Treasurer and of the Chamberlain of England; and 12s was spent on 'ane puire manes heid [a duster] for dichting doune the haill mouse webbis [spiders' webs] throw the haill pallace'.

After the departure of Charles and his retinue before the end of the year, the palace was left once more in the hands of the hereditary keeper, whose family are recorded in 1648 occupying the second floor of the new north range.

Following the execution of the king in 1649, the Scots proclaimed his son as Charles II, and Oliver Cromwell invaded the country. He defeated the Scots army at Dunbar in September 1650 and spent the winter at Linlithgow, installing himself in the 'new work', while his troops camped in the peel. The fortifications erected around the palace probably followed the line of Edward I's *pele*, but would have consisted of banks and ditches designed to be defended by artillery.

After the restoration of Charles II (1660–85), a warrant was issued in January 1663 to the earl of Linlithgow to have the English defences levelled, the work to be undertaken at the expense of the burgh. In 1668, the palace itself was described by John Lauder, Lord Fountainhall, as formerly 'werie magnificent' but 'now for the most part ruinous'. Captain John Slezer's engraving of 1678, however, shows that the palace was still roofed; and graffiti made by the cooks in the court kitchen in 1685 and 1687 show that it was then still in use. James, duke of Albany and York, the brother of Charles II, later to become King James VII, is known to have made use of the palace while acting as Commissioner to the Scottish Parliament in 1679 and 1680–2.

# THE JACOBITE REBELLION
# AND THE RUIN OF THE PALACE

Wooden panel, bearing the Royal Arms, dating to around 1530, salvaged from the ruined palace after the fire of 1746.

*Right:*
Prince Charles Edward Stuart, the Young Pretender, who stayed in the palace in 1745 (painting by Antonio David).

T HE PALACE'S CONNECTIONS with the House of Stuart continued even after the 'Glorious Revolution' of 1688–9 which removed James VII from the throne. In 1715, the keeper, James, fifth earl of Linlithgow and fourth earl of Callander, supported James Edward Stuart, the 'Old Pretender', and forfeited his titles and the hereditary keepership as a result. In 1745, Prince Charles Edward Stuart was the last of that house to stay in the building. In January 1746, however, troops of the duke of Cumberland's army were billeted in the palace. On 1 February, when they marched out, fires were left burning which soon caught hold of the building and burnt it out.

Since 1746, the palace has remained unroofed and uninhabited. Nevertheless, a succession of keepers was appointed who, except during the years 1799–1803, held the

The palace from the north, drawn by M. Bouquet, 1849.

title and its associated rents and perquisites until 1853, when, on the death of Admiral Sir Thomas Livingstone leaving no heir, the duty of collecting the rents (valued at £400 a year) and maintaining the park, or 'peel' as it has come to be called, was entrusted to Her Majesty's Commissioners of Woods and Forests. A report by James McNab of the Royal Botanic Gardens in Edinburgh gave recommendations at that time for levelling and landscaping the mounds of earth and rubbish lying around the palace and for reclaiming the marshy area on the east where the town drains entered the loch.

In 1874 care of the palace passed to the Commissioners for Works and Public Buildings. Various proposals for re-roofing it for use as a museum or law courts were made in the 1890s. In 1906 the fireplace in the great hall was restored; and a programme of clearance and consolidation was carried through over the next three decades.

Today the palace is cared for on behalf of the Secretary of State for Scotland by Historic Buildings and Monuments (Scottish Development Department). The peel is administered as one of the Royal Parks, and for this reason, like the park of Holyroodhouse, it has its own park police force.

William Augustus, duke of Cumberland (painting by the studio of Sir Joshua Reynolds, c1758–60).

The fireplace in the great hall, restored in 1906.

# LINLITHGOW PALACE – CHRONOLOGICAL CHART OF OWNERS AND OFFICERS

## Kings and Queens

1124–53 David I
1153–65 Malcolm IV
1165–1214 William I
1214–49 Alexander II
1249–86 Alexander III
1286–90 Margaret
1290–1306 John
1306–29 Robert I
1329–71 David II
1371–90 Robert II
1390–1406 Robert III
1406–37 James I
1437–60 James II
1460–88 James III
1488–1513 James IV
1513–42 James V
1542–67 Mary
1567–1625 James VI
1625–49 Charles I
1649–85 Charles II
1685–89 James VII
1689–1702 William & Mary
1702–1714 Anne
1714–27 George I
1727–60 George II
1760–1820 George III
1820–30 George IV
1830–37 William IV
1837–1901 Victoria

## Other Royal Owners

1263–86 Dowery of Princess Margaret of Flanders
1286–94 Sold to Guy, count of Flanders
1291, 1296, 1298–1307 Held by Edward I of England
1307–14 Held for Edward II of England
1314 Abandoned by English
1334–37 Possibly held by English
1471 Dowery of Queen Margaret of Denmark
1503–13 Dowery of Queen Margaret Tudor
1542–54 Residence of Lord Governor, the second earl of Arran
1551–60 For use of Queen Mary of Guise (Queen Regent from 1554)
1589 Dowery of Queen Anne of Denmark

## Sheriffs

(1162) unnamed
(pre-1263) Roger of Moubray
(1288) William of St Clair

## Keepers and Constables

(1302) Sir Archibald Livingstone
1302 William of Felton
(1309–12) Sir Peter Libaud
(1337)–[c1340] John Carnys/Cairns
(1406–21) Angus de Camera
1425–34 John de Waltoun
1434 Sir Robert de Wedale, abbot of Culross
1434–37 Robert of Livingstone
(1446) Reginald de Craufurde
(1450) John Weir
(1454) James Clerksoune
(1458) Nicolas Henrysoun
(1461–70) John of Kincade
(1487)–88 Anselm Sersandreis
1488–91 George Packle
1491–95 Sir William Knollis/of St John
1495–[97] James Akinheide
1497–[1501] Andrew Caveris, abbot of Lindores
(1501) Robert Lundy of Balgony (?)
1502–03 Henry Forest
1503–[04] Sir John Ramsay of Trarinyeane
(1504–14) Sir Alexander McCulloch of Myretoun
1526–37 Sir James Hamilton of Fynnart
1537–38 Sir Thomas Johnston
1538–40 Sir James Hamilton of Fynnart
1540 Sir Thomas Johnston
1540–43 William Danielston
1543 Robert Hamilton of Briggis
(1543) Matthew Hamilton of Millburn
(1545) Andrew Hamilton of Lethame
(1550) Robert Hamilton of Briggis
1567 Andrew Ferrier
1567–71 Robert Melville of Murdocairney
1571–80 Capt Andrew Lamby
1580– Robert Stewart
1587–91 Sir Lewis Bellenden
1599–1621 Alexander Livingstone, first earl of Linlithgow
1621–27 Sir William Bellenden of Broughton
1627–42 Alexander, second earl of Linlithgow
1642–90 George, third earl of Linlithgow
1690–95 George, fourth earl of Linlithgow
1695–1715 James, fifth earl of Linlithgow and fourth earl of Callander
1715–19 vacant
1719–42 James, first duke of Montrose
1743–77 James Glen Esq of Longcroft
1777–99 Douglas, eighth duke of Hamilton
1799–1803 vacant
1803–53 Sir Thomas Livingstone
1853–74 HM Commissioners of Woods and Forests
1874– HM Commissioners of Works and Public Buildings

## Masters of Works (other than Keeper) and Masons

1302 Master James of St George (MW)
1302 Thomas of Houghton and Adam of Glasham (MW)
1304 John of Wrocwardyn (MW)
(1448) John Holmes (MW)
(1469–70) Henry Livingstone (MW)
1502–03 Thomas Forest (MW)
(1504) Nicholas Jackson (M)
(1511–13) Stephen Balty/Bawtee (M)
(1513) James Carvour (M)
1534– Thomas French (M)
(1535–36) Sir Thomas Johnston (MW)
(1550–52) Sir John Polwart (MW)
(1567–79) Sir William McDowell (MW)
1619–21 William Wallace (MM)

## Key

| | |
|---|---|
| ( ) | = Minimal Date |
| [ ] | = Assumed Dates |
| (MW) | = Master of Works |
| (MM) | = Master Mason |
| (M) | = Mason |

Printed in Scotland for HMSO by (56901)
Dd287186 HF4781 C127 4/89